# Contents

# Foreword

Welcome to this new piano series designed for today's pianist. A variety of piano music from blues, jazz and pop idioms, folk songs, Native American songs, hymn arrangements, Christmas Carols and classical music are included in this series. In addition to a wide variety of musical styles, each book will include exercises, palindromes and a duet.

Each book in the series is a complete integrated piano course which combines repertoire from many periods of music (from Bach to Kabalevsky) with music by favorite American composers.

The series also provides a thorough study of scales, cadences, arpeggios and musical terms. Theory studies are incorporated throughout the series and a short quiz concludes each book.

As you complete each book, I hope you will look forward to going on to the next book in the series through *Book Five*. As you progress, should you need additional piano solos, you may obtain the book at the same level of *The Great Literature Series* also available from Mel Bay Publications, Inc. This series offers eight graded books of supplementary piano literature for your enjoyment, all containing original compositions by the masters.

Music is a universal language, and in this series of books you will find what I feel is the most interesting and enjoyable music available. I hope that you will agree...and that your interest in music and playing the piano will last a lifetime.

**Gail Smith**

# History of the Piano

As we "celebrate the piano" at the beginning of the new millennium, it is hard to believe that the grand piano is the product of a 300-hundred year evolutionary process. Playing the piano has always been a popular pastime and the appearance of a grand piano in one's home is certainly a symbol of culture.

## Organ

In Greece, over 2000 years ago, the first organ, the hydraulis, used both water and air pressure applied by a hand pump to create it's sound. The hydraulis provided music at ceremonies and gladiatorial events during the Roman Empire.

## Clavichord

While its origin's are obscure, the clavichord evolved as early as the thirteenth century. The clavichord creates a very soft, delicate sound ranging from pianissimo to mezzo piano. When a clavichord key is pressed, a metal rod with a blunt chisel tip called a "tangent" strikes a string or pair of strings. The portion of the strings to the right of the tangent vibrates only as long as the key is pressed. While the clavichord had no pedals, a player with a sensitive touch could raise the pitch of a note by applying more pressure and even produce a vibrato effect. Clavichords made before 1720 had fewer strings than keys, as more than one tangent might strike the same string. Such instruments were called "fretted" clavichords. Daniel Tob introduced the "fretless" clavichord in 1720. Fretless clavichords featured a separate pair of strings for each note/key.

## Harpsichord

Following the clavichord by at least 100 years, the harpsichord was often a large and elaborately decorated instrument. Typically, the keys of the harpsichord were made of ivory, while using pearl on the more extravagant models. The harpsichord was an altogether different instrument than the clavichord. Queen Elizabeth played the harpsichord, inspiring the instrument's first triumph in England.

The strings of the harpsichord are mechanically plucked, unlike the clavichord which is pressure struck. The primary part of the harpsichord's action is the "jack", a short vertical piece of wood armed with a plectrum made from either crow quill or leather. The jack rests on the end of an extended lever of the key, which when depressed, causes the quill to pluck the string. The jack falls back down again when the key is released. Several jacks might be activated by the same key, producing a slightly different tone depending on the material used for the plectrum. There might also be several strings to each key, allowing the playing of octaves with a single key.

The harpsichord had two manual keyboards and many hand stops by which the various jacks and strings could be brought into play making some degree of registration possible.

Bach and his contemporaries used the registers of the harpsichord less than most modern harpsichord players. In the early harpsichord, the change of registers was made exclusively by using hand stops, not by pedals, which are used in most of the modern reproductions, limiting the free and frequent change of stops.

The greatest deficiency of the harpsichord is its inability to produce any gradation of sound by applying a lighter or heavier touch. The clavichord approaches the pianoforte's strengths more closely than the harpsichord, because it can produce a gradation of sound even though the range is limited.

The desire to combine the clavichord's power of accentuation, crescendo, diminuendo, and cantabile with the force and brilliance of the harpsichord set the stage for the introduction of the next generation of keyboard instruments—the pianoforte.

### Cristofori's Piano

In 1698, Bartolommeo Cristofori began work on a special keyboard instrument that could play both more loudly and more softly, substituting hammers for quills. By 1709, Cristofori had made four pianofortes in Florence, Italy. Cristofori died in 1731.

The pianoforte, during its emergence in the second half of the eighteenth century was received with both hostility and enthusiasm. The Germans, unwilling to give up their beloved clavichord, rejected it most persistently; the French remained skeptical, but the English adopted it wholeheartedly.

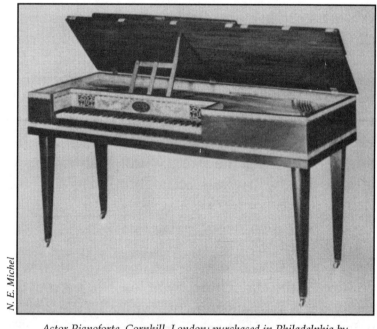

*Astor Pianoforte, Cornhill, London; purchased in Philadelphia by Thomas Jefferson in 1800 for $264.00.*

There were earlier attempts at creating the piano, but it was not until Cristofori that the principle of the hammer-action really worked. This new invention was called the pianoforte because notes could be played softly or loudly depending on how hard the keys were struck. Cristofori's mechanism was very clever. When any hammer struck a string, it returned immediately, leaving the string free to vibrate. Cristofori's mechanism was also equipped with dampers, which fell at once upon the string and stopped its vibration, ending the sound when the player's finger lifted from the key.

### Gottfried Silbermann

The German organ builder Gottfried Silbermann built a modified, improved piano and the King of Prussia, Frederick the Great purchased over a dozen of them. J. S. Bach took advantage of the opportunity to play the new German-made pianos while visiting with the King.

Creative Keyboard Presents

# Celebrate
## the Piano

## Book 1

## by Gail Smith

1 2 3 4 5 6 7 8 9 0

**CHECK OUT CREATIVE KEYBOARD'S** *FREE WEBZINE* @ **www.creativekeyboard.com**

*Visit us on the Web at www.melbay.com — E-mail us at email@melbay.com*

Alex

Erika

*This book is dedicated to
my Granddaughters,
Alex and Erika.*

## The Upright Piano

This piano had an entirely new form with the strings descending below the keyboard. Frederici of Gera in Saxony made the earliest upright grand in 1745; Frederici also invented the square grand.

## The Square Piano

John Behrend of Philadelphia, Pennsylvania built the first piano ever made in America in 1774. The framework of Behrend's square piano was made of wood, which was not strong enough to endure the tension of the strings.

*N. E. Michel*

*Bradbury Upright Piano No. 15561 used in the White House; gift of Bradbury Piano Co., now in the Hayes Library, presented by the Ohio Girls' Club of Washington, D.C.*

The tuning block was inverted in the new square piano: that is, the strings were vertical instead of horizontal. These elegant pianos were beautiful pieces of furniture. Carved wooden legs accented the cabinet. John Isaac Hawkins, of Boardertown, New Jersey, patented two new features for the piano: the use of coil-wound strings for the bass, and a sostenete pedal that set hammers in motion via rollers. Hawkins' piano was first played in public at the Franklin Institute in Philadelphia in 1802.

*N. E. Michel*

*Steinway & Sons Square Piano in the home of Andrew Johnson; bought for his daughter in 1868; used at the White House.*

## The Metal-Frame Piano

Piano makers had a problem with the wire used for the strings—if the wire was too thin, it couldn't withstand the blow of the hammers; if the wire was too thick, the wooden cabinets weren't strong enough to support the tension. A young Scottish tuner named William Allen, while working at Stodart's, an English family of pianoforte makers in London, produced an upper frame combining plates of iron and brass bound together by wooden crossbars, thus bearing the pull of the strings. Allen patented these changes on January 15, 1820. Alpheus Babcock made the first full cast-iron plate in 1825. In 1831, Allen patented his invention of the cast-iron frame, which combined the string-plate, iron bars and wrest plank in one casting. Conrad Meyer of Philadelphia claimed to have invented a metal frame in 1832. It seems that all three men, Allen, Babcock and Meyer each built and modified the square grand piano by incorporating a metal-frame at or around the same time.

## The Grand Piano

In 1835, Jonas Chickering combined the overstringing* with a metal frame in one casting. Steinway & Sons made further improvements on the piano in 1859 by dividing the overstringing into two crossings and by putting the longer bass strings at an angle across some of the shorter strings. Within two decades, Steinway & Sons had patented close to twenty improvements in the grand piano.

While undergoing several improvements, it took the pianoforte about one century to replace both the harpsichord and the clavichord as the keyboard of choice. The three instruments have different qualities, but rarely does one home suitably hold all three. The music composed during the height of each instrument's popularity accentuates the special qualities of the respective instruments, making the harpsichord and the clavichord irreplaceable.

The soundboard of a modern grand piano is made of spruce that may have taken up to five hundred years to grow. The hammers are voiced to perfection. The harder the hammer, the shorter the tone; the softer the hammer, the longer the note carries.

There are twelve thousand parts to a grand piano. According to George Bernard Shaw, "The pianoforte is the most important of all musical instruments; its invention was to music what the invention of the printing press was to poetry".

What better way to *"Celebrate the Piano"* than to begin lessons or start practicing again, learning pieces by the great piano composers?

---

*The universally adopted method of placing the longer bass strings at a diagonal over the shorter strings to increase their length and create a fuller tone.

THE
MUSIC
HOUSE

If you intend the piano to learn,
Great care must be taken, as you will discern;
Your position must by with grace and ease,
Mind what I say now, if you please.

In the middle of the keyboard you must sit,
So the lowest or the highest note you can get,
Your seat should be at a proper height,
With your elbows a little above keyboard,
That's right!

Dear Piano Student:

As you begin your study of piano
one of the most important things to
do is ... practice daily.

"Perhaps the most valuable result of
all education is the ability to make
yourself do the thing you have
to do, when it ought to be done,
whether you like it or not."
...Thomas Huxley

"Beginnings are alike, it is ends which differ.
One drop falls, lasts, and dries up, ♪
Another begins a River." ♪

My hope is that you will enjoy music,
learn to read notes and play all the songs
in the book.

GAIL SMITH

# The Piano Keyboard

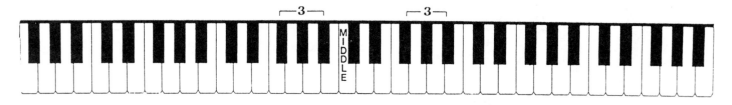

The keyboard has **white** and **black** keys.
The black keys are in sets of **2's and 3's.**

When you play down the piano keyboard,

The notes sound lower and lower.

With your left hand, find and play all the groups of three black keys.

When you play up on the piano keyboard,

The notes sound higher and higher.

With your right hand, find and play the groups of three black keys.

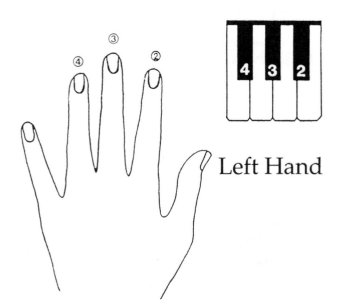

Left Hand

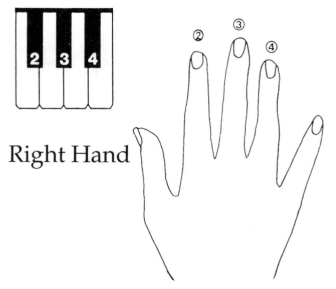

Right Hand

# Indian Trails

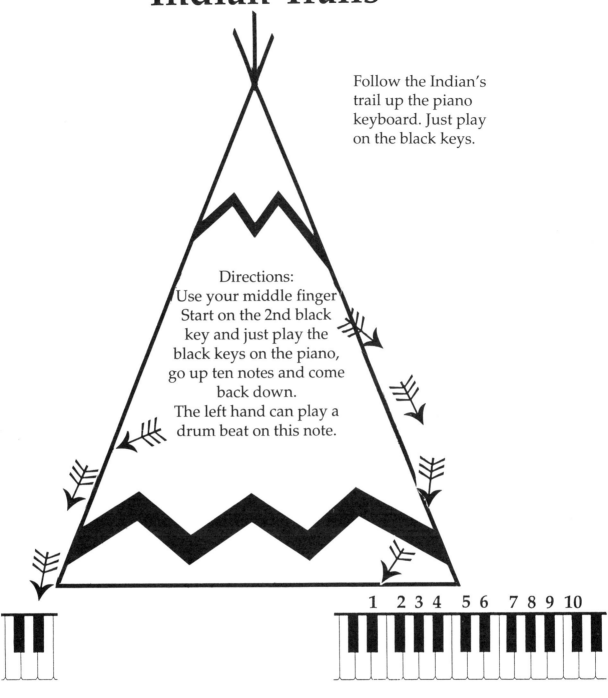

Follow the Indian's trail up the piano keyboard. Just play on the black keys.

Directions:
Use your middle finger
Start on the 2nd black key and just play the black keys on the piano, go up ten notes and come back down.
The left hand can play a drum beat on this note.

1 2 3 4 5 6 7 8 9 10

# Follow
# The Indian Trail

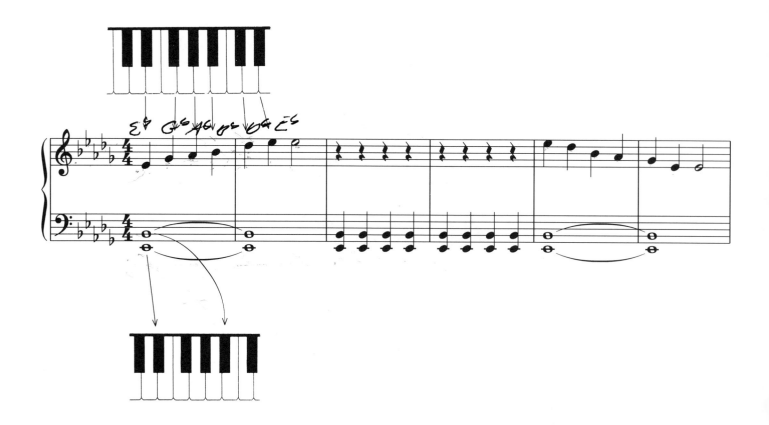

Low E flat        Low B flat

Keep playing the left hand chord shown above and continue playing only the black notes in the right hand.

# Clap The Following
# Time Lines

Time Line

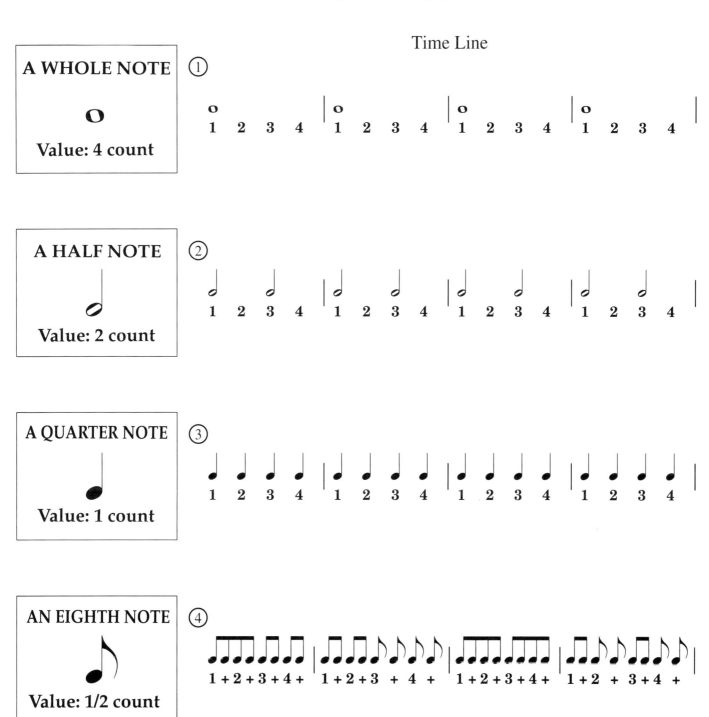

The note at the very top of the piano with 88 keys is a C. Middle C is the fourth C going up from the left side of the piano.

Find and play all the C's.

This is Middle C as a whole note:

This is Middle C as a dotted half note:

This is Middle C as a half note:

This is Middle C as a quarter note:

This is Middle C as a running eighth note:

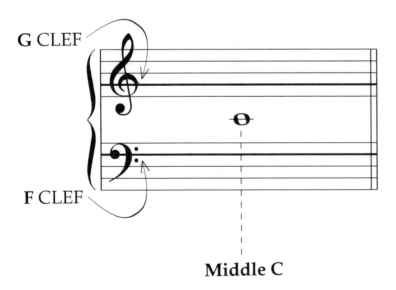

G CLEF

F CLEF

**Middle C**

# Playing The Piano
# Is Grand

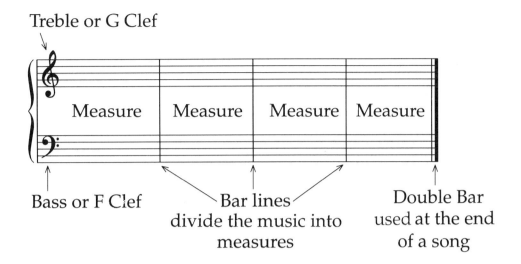

Treble or G Clef

Measure   Measure   Measure   Measure

Bass or F Clef

Bar lines
divide the music into
measures

Double Bar
used at the end
of a song

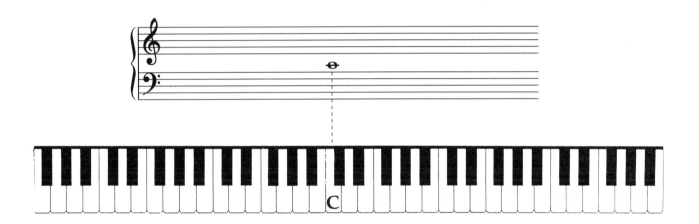

C

Are these notes on a Line or a Space?

S    L    L    S    S    L

D    E    E    A    D    B

A    E    C    G    F    D

C    A    D    A    C    G

B    G    F    C    A    D

There are
Five Lines

There are
Four Spaces

LINES        SPACES

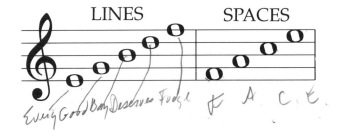

Every Good Boy Deserves Fudge        F  A  C  E

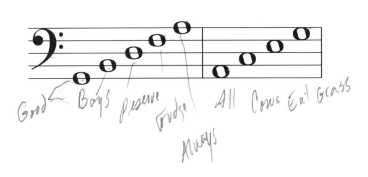

Good Boys Deserve Fudge    All Cows Eat Grass
Always

16

# Walking Down The Street

## (Keep Counting 1,2,3,4)

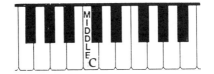

Gail Smith

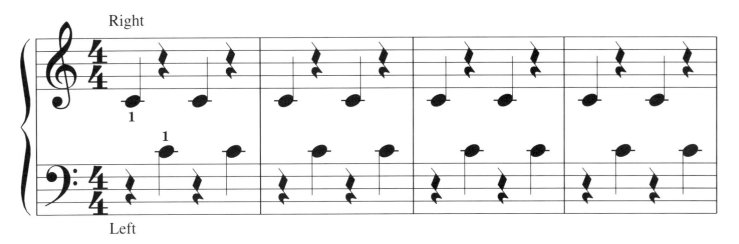

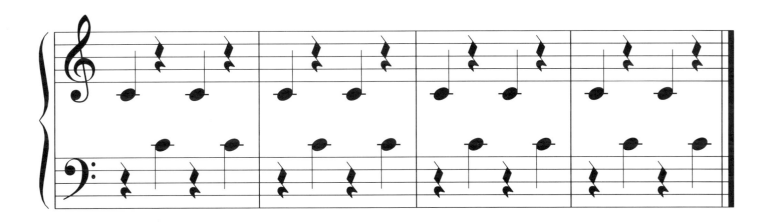

# Marching

Count all the way please,
each half note gets two counts.

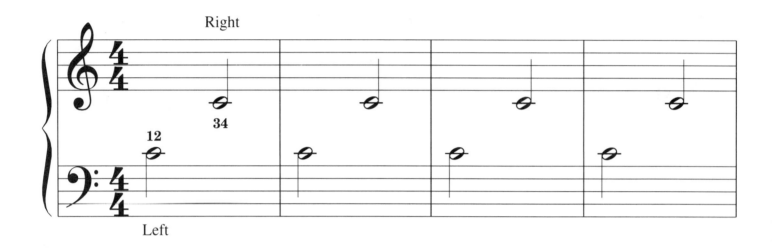

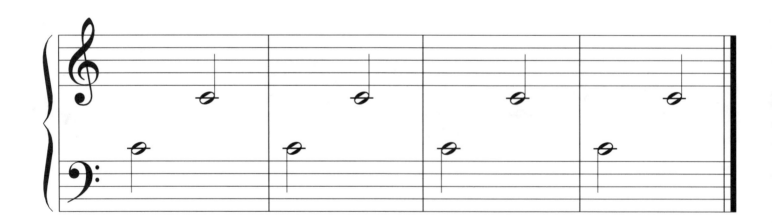

# Snapping

Gail Smith

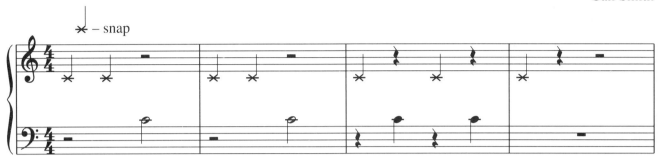

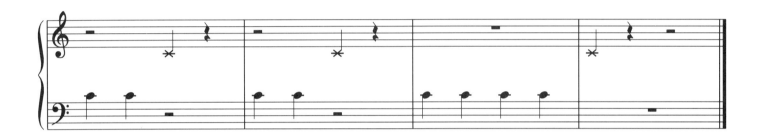

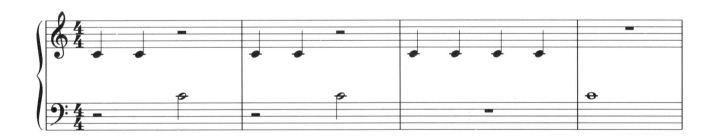

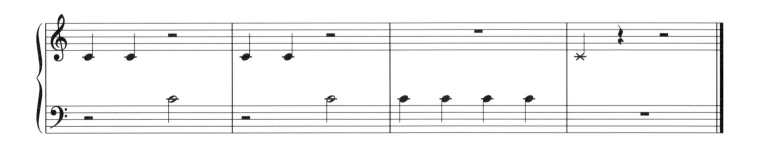

# In The Beginning

Gail Smith

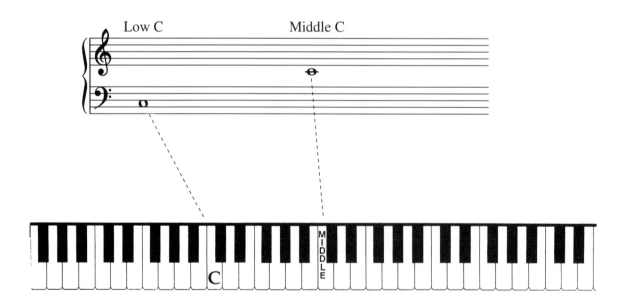

Draw the following notes and know their names and values:

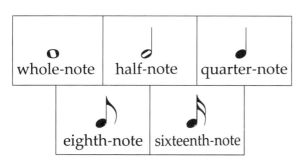

Draw a row of whole notes

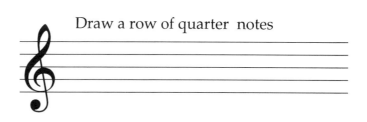

Draw a row of half notes

Draw a row of quarter notes

Draw a row of eighth notes

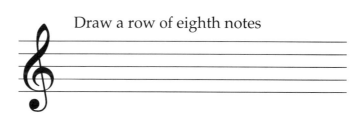

# Swimming To The Shore

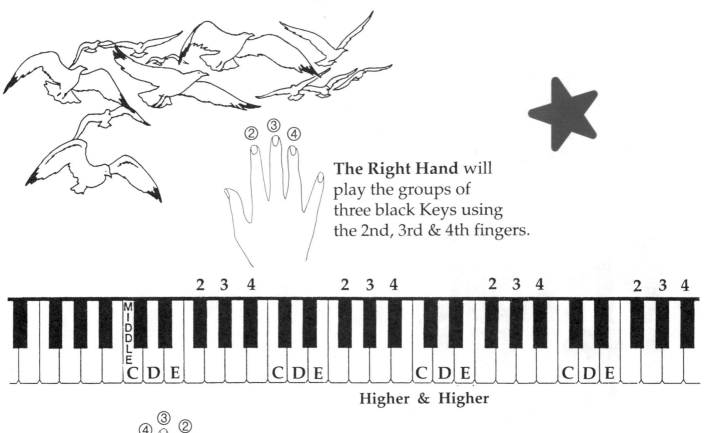

**The Right Hand** will play the groups of three black Keys using the 2nd, 3rd & 4th fingers.

Higher & Higher

**The Left Hand** will play the three white notes, C, D & E using the 4th, 3rd & 2nd fingers.

Hold the Pedal on the right side down with your right foot for the **entire** song.

**Final Directions :**
Alternate using the left and right hands playing up and down the keyboard using just the notes marked for each hand. You may play the black notes as clusters or separately. Have fun!

# Underwater Sounds

Gail Smith

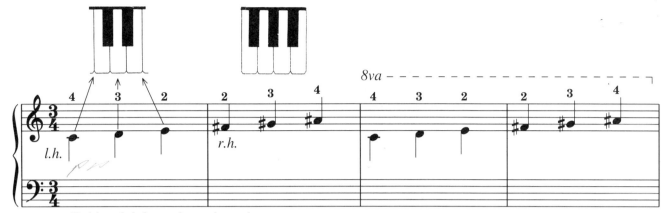

Hold pedal down throughout the song

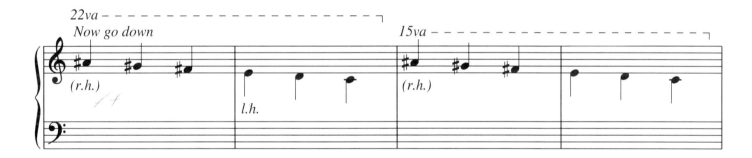

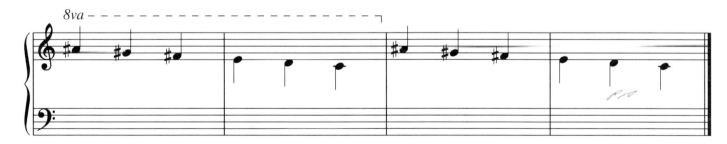

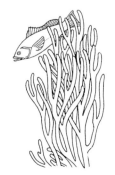

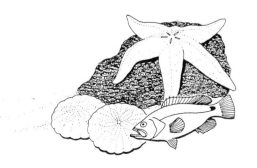

# Song Of The Sea

Gail Smith

Find your
new note

B C D

Circle the dynamic sign
that describes the picture.

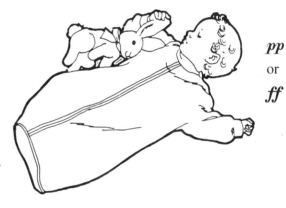

*pp*

or

*ff*

# Dynamic Signs

There are marks of expression that you should know,
So that all music can tastefully go,
They are called dynamics, and of many kind,
Which you , as you progress, will find.

**P,** for Piano, play softly,
**F,** somewhat louder, stands for forte,
**Double P,** Pianissimo, quite delicate,
**Double F,** for Fortissmo, the sound becomes louder than forte.

Circle the dynamic sign
that describes the picture.

*ff*

or

*p*

| *p* | *pp* | *f* | *ff* |

# Day And Night

Introducing the note D

Gail Smith

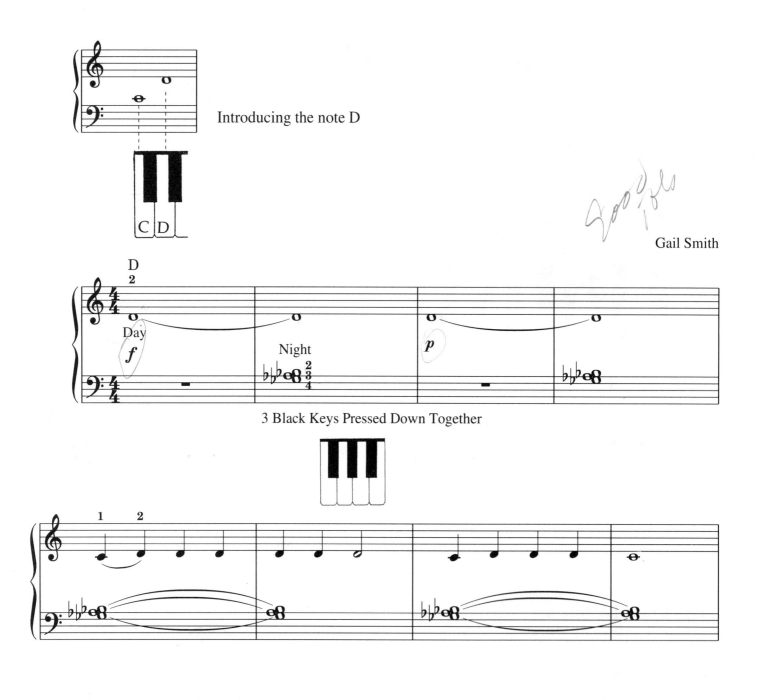

3 Black Keys Pressed Down Together

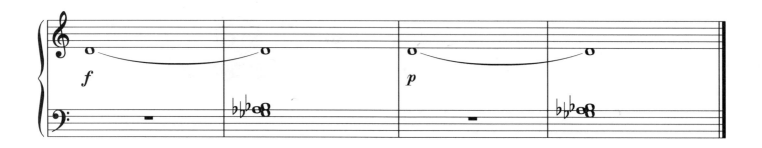

# Resting By The Lake

| | QUARTER REST | HALF REST | WHOLE REST | |
|---|---|---|---|---|
| RESTS | | | | |
| NOTE value | 1 | 1, 2 | 1,2,3,4 | |

There are signs of silence, called rests.
They tell us when and how many beats to be silent.

Gail Smith

# Runnning on A& E

 *count aloud*

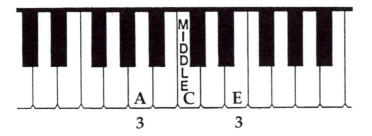

Eighth note ♪ equals half a count. Play TWO eighth notes ♫ to ONE count.

*fast*

Let's Run, Allegro is the musical term.

*medium*

Now Walk, Andante is the musical term.

Please Slow Down, Lento means slow.

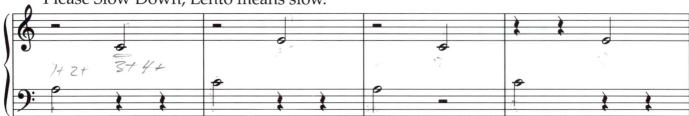

Very Slow now. Adagio. Stand Still, Rest.

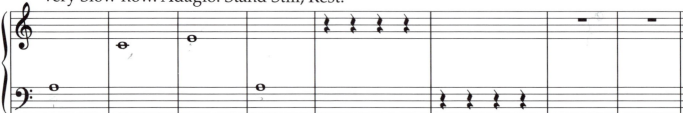

# The Musical Alphabet

A, B, C, D, and E, F, G,
Are names of the notes, alphabetically,
These first seven letters you sure must learn,
To the staff you next your attention must turn.

The staff consists of five lines and four spaces,
And notes are written on all places.

LINES                           SPACES

| E | G | B | D | F | F | A | C | E |
| G | B | D | F | A | A | C | E | G |

Write your name on the line below and find the musical
letters in your name, then draw them in the staff below.

29

# The Game Room

Example

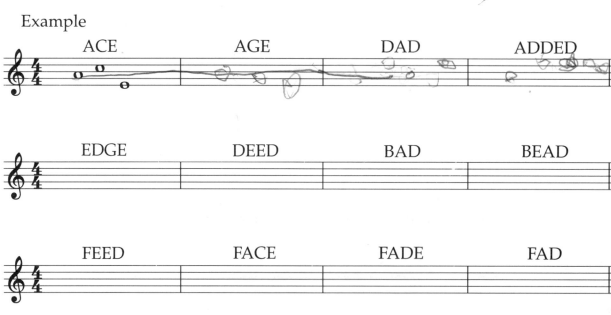

|  ACE | AGE | DAD | ADDED |
| EDGE | DEED | BAD | BEAD |
| FEED | FACE | FADE | FAD |
| BAGGAGE | BEG | CABBAGE | BEEF |

Draw the musical notes found in these sixteen words on their space or line.

Study the musical alphabet on the preceding page.

# Hot Cross Buns

Remember,
Forte means Loud

*Count loud*

Piano means Soft

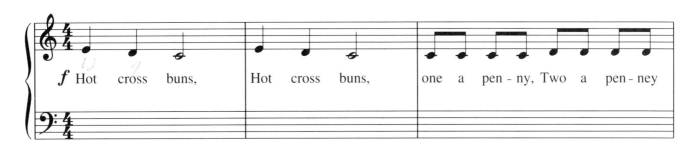

f Hot cross buns, | Hot cross buns, | one a pen - ny, Two a pen - ney

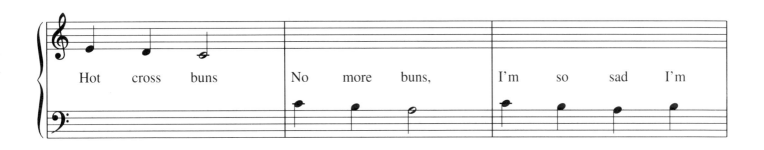

Hot cross buns | No more buns, | I'm so sad I'm

on a di - et star - ting now, so | no more buns.

# When I Survey The Wondrous Cross

Lowell Mason
(1792–1872)

**Isaac Watts**

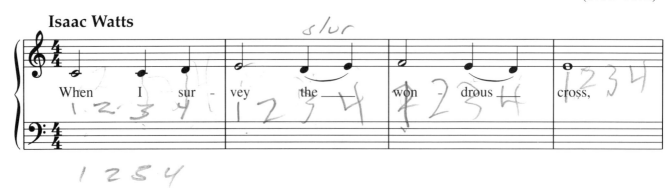

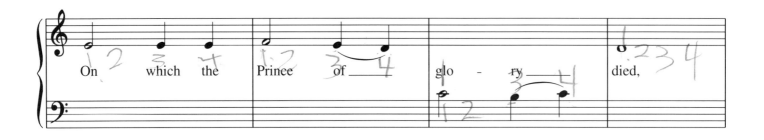

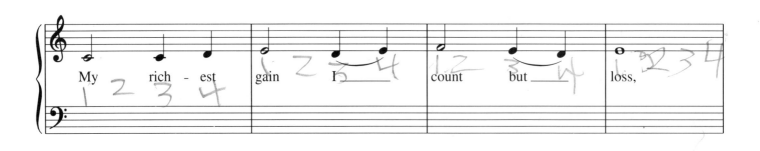

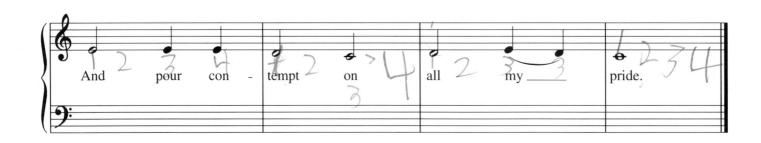

# Three Patterns
# of Notes

Examples:

### Notes that repeat
1.

### Notes that step
2.

### Notes that skip
3.

In the quiz, fill in the answer:
repeated, step or skip notes.

Identify these patterns and notes:

 *repeat*

 *skip*

 *step*

 *repeat*

 *step*

 *step*

# Old MacDonald

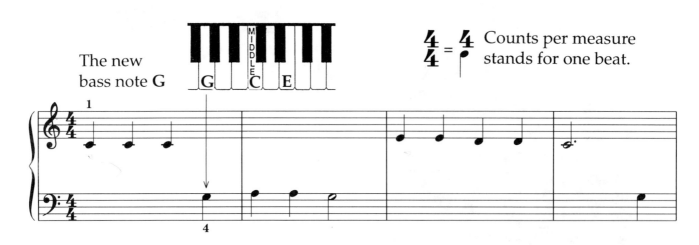

The new bass note G

$\frac{4}{4} = \frac{4}{\text{♩}}$ Counts per measure stands for one beat.

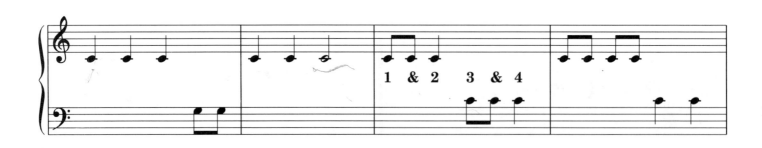

# Introducing Time Signatures

Each measure of music has a specified number of **beats** or **counts**. The numbers at the beginning of a piece will indicate **how many beats** in a measure, and **what kind of a note** gets a beat.

**2** Top number = 2 beats in each measure.
**4** Bottom number = A quarter note (♩) gets one beat.

**3** Top number = 3 beats in each measure.
**4** Bottom number = A quarter note (♩) gets one beat.

**4** Top number = 4 beats in each measure.
**4** Bottom number = A quarter note (♩) gets one beat.

**6** Top number = 6 beats in each measure.
**8** Bottom number = An eighth note (♪) gets one beat.

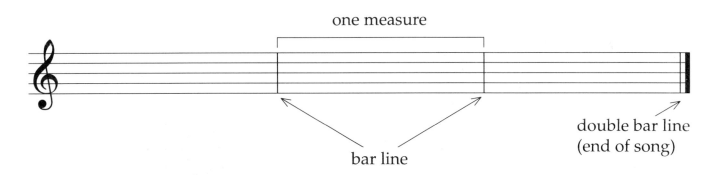

one measure

bar line

double bar line
(end of song)

From one bar line to another is a full measure. At the beginning of each song, the Time Signature will appear. Watch for it!

# The Clock

## Time Signatures

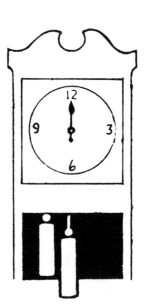

The **TIME SIGNATURE** shows how many
beats are in each measure in the music.

$$\frac{3}{4} = \frac{3}{\text{♩}}$$  Counts per measure
stands for one beat

**The TOP number tells how many beats are in each measure.**
**The BOTTOM number tells what kind of note = 1 beat. (4 = ♩)**

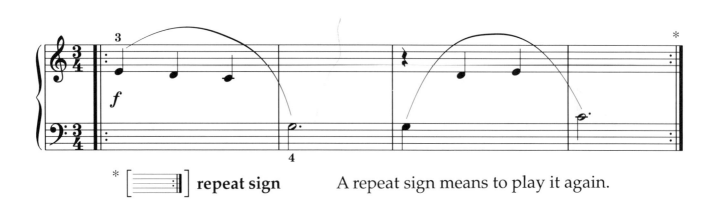

\* [𝄆 𝄇] **repeat sign**     A repeat sign means to play it again.

# Pop! Goes The Weasel

**DOTTED HALF NOTE = 3 BEATS**           ♩. = **3 BEATS**

The **DOTTED HALF NOTE holds for 3 beats**. When clapping rhythms with a dotted half note, you can say **"half-note-dot"**

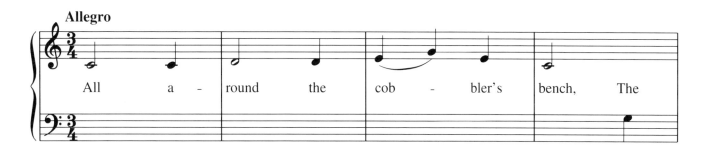

All  a - round  the  cob - bler's  bench,  The

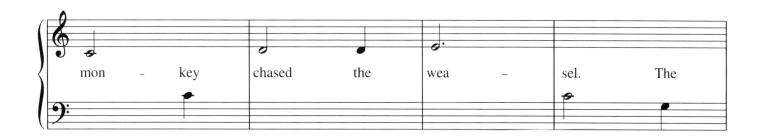

mon - key  chased  the  wea - sel.  The

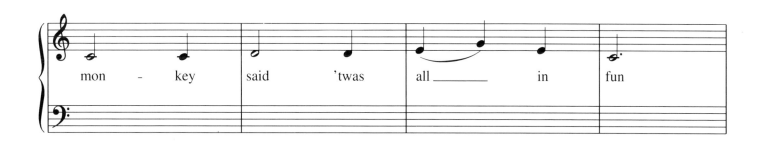

mon - key  said  'twas  all _____ in  fun

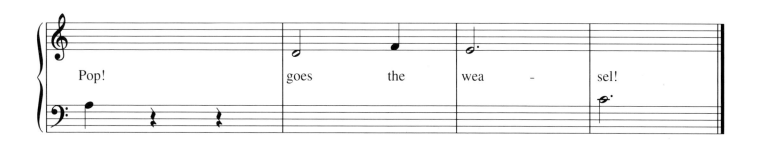

Pop!  goes  the  wea - sel!

Let's play the theme from a Symphony

# The Theme From Haydn's Surprise Symphony

This melody is the theme from Haydn's "Surprise" Symphony. The word "symphony" comes from two Greek words and means just "sounding together". You find the "sym" also in words like "sympathy" and "symmetry," and the "phony" occurs in "telephone" and "microphone". Usually a large orchestra has at least sixty players Franz Joseph Haydn, who lived from 1732 - 1809 is called the "Father of the Symphony".

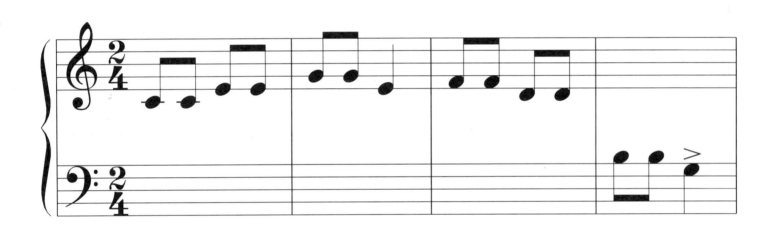

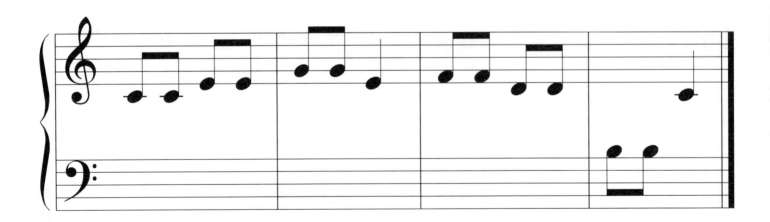

# Ode To Joy

Beethoven

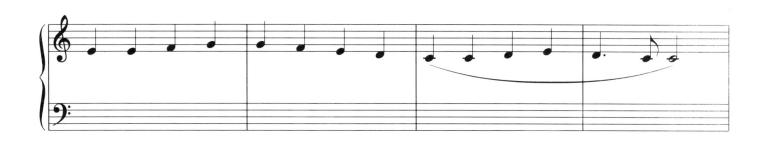

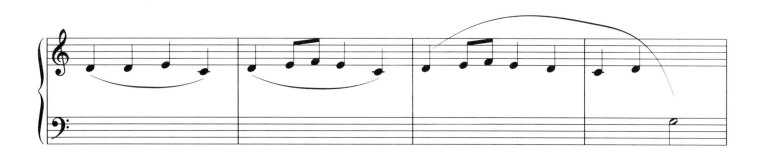

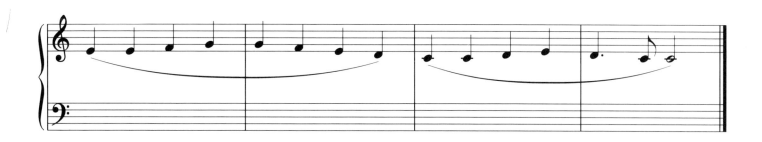

# Rain, Rain!

Playing staccato means to play quick, detached notes.

A dot over or under a note means staccato.

Gail Smith

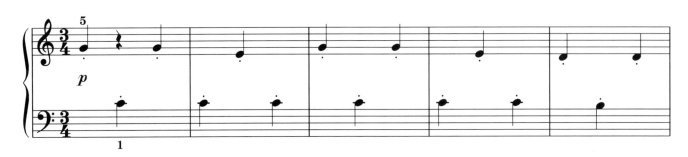

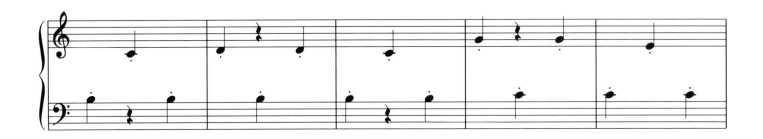

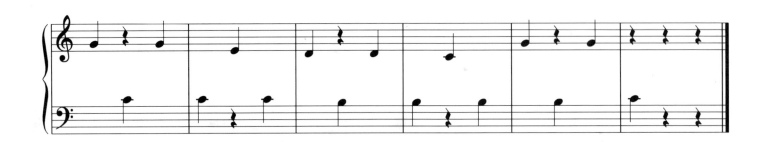

# The Quacking Ducks

The interval of a 3rd

Gail Smith

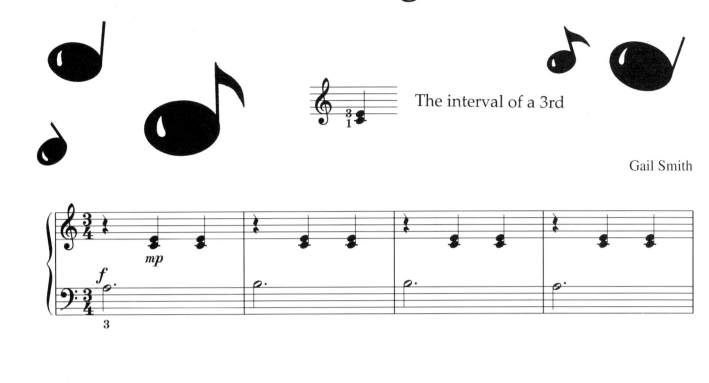

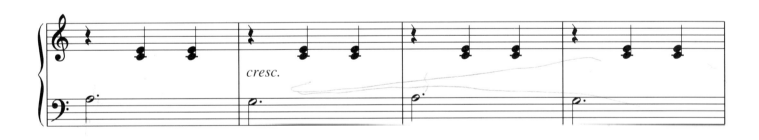

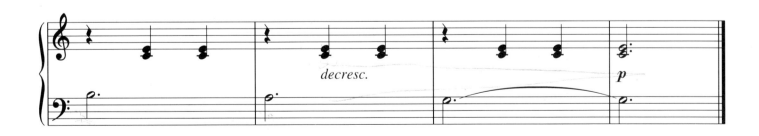

# Bingo

# The Wind Blows

Gail Smith

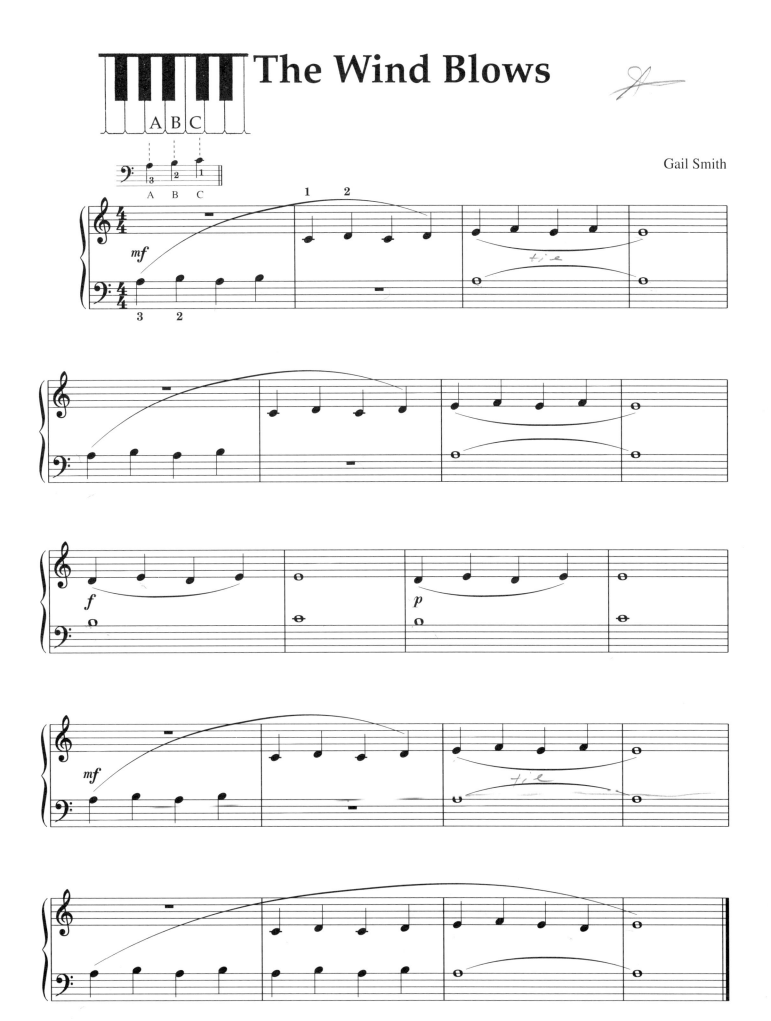

# The Face In Space

Gail Smith

Middle C

44

# Message From Space

CIRCLE ONLY THE SPACES OF THE TREBLE CLEF
(IN THEIR GROUP OF FOUR)

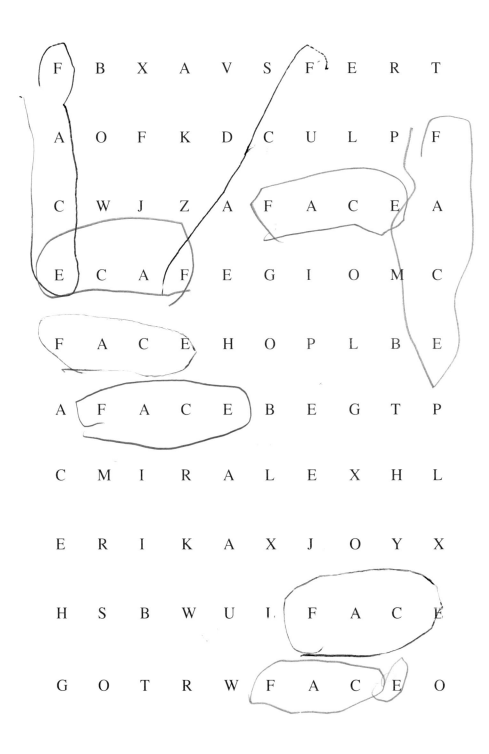

|   |   |   |   |   |   |   |   |   |   |
|---|---|---|---|---|---|---|---|---|---|
| F | B | X | A | V | S | F | E | R | T |
| A | O | F | K | D | C | U | L | P | F |
| C | W | J | Z | A | F | A | C | E | A |
| E | C | A | F | E | G | I | O | M | C |
| F | A | C | E | H | O | P | L | B | E |
| A | F | A | C | E | B | E | G | T | P |
| C | M | I | R | A | L | E | X | H | L |
| E | R | I | K | A | X | J | O | Y | X |
| H | S | B | W | U | I | F | A | C | E |
| G | O | T | R | W | F | A | C | E | O |

How many Space Stations
did you find?_____

45

# The Stars

| | | |
|---|---|---|
| *mp* ] | **medium soft** | *m* is an abbreviation for mezzo, |
| *mf* ] | **medium loud** | Italian for "medium" |

Gail Smith

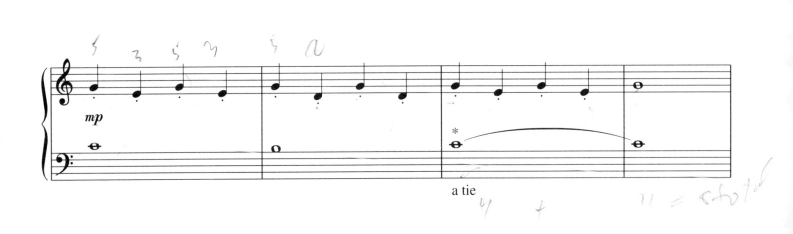

a tie

\* A TIE is a curved line connecting two successive notes.

# Lullaby Of The Birds

Gail Smith

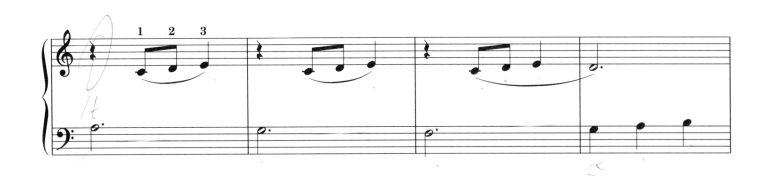

# Look For Cabbage

How many times does the word "Cabbage" appear?

Gail Smith

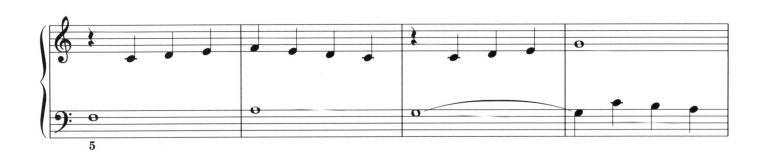

# Mary Had A Little Lamb

This song is a "Semordnilap". It can be played forward and then sounds different when it is played backwards. When you play this song backwards, you will recognize the song as, "Mary Had A Little Lamb".

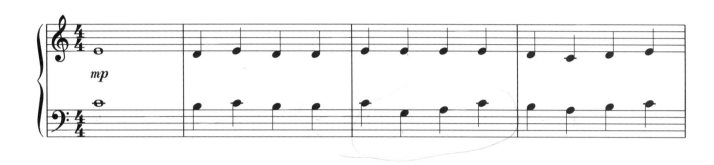

# My Favorite Duet

(The teacher will play this part)

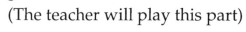

**Secondo**

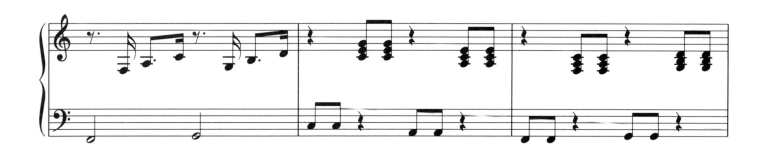

1st ending     2nd ending

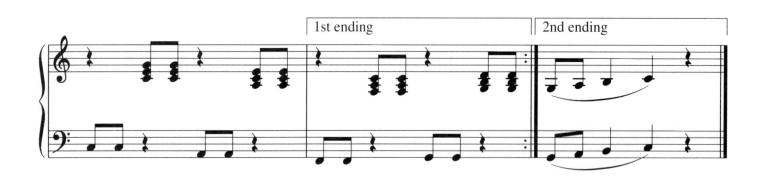

# My Favorite Duet

**Primo**

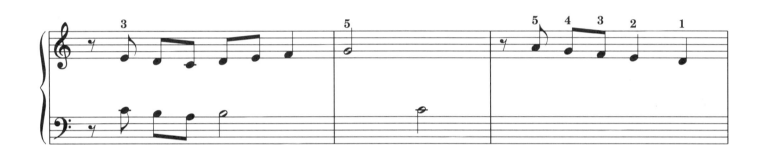

# The Pledge To The American Flag

Fill in the missing letters by naming the notes.

I Ple_d_ g _e_ _ll _ _i_ n _ to th_

_l _ o _ th _ Unit _ _ St _ t _ s

o _ _m _ ri _ _ _n _ to th _

R _ pu _ li _ _ or whi _ h it St _ n _ s

on _ _ n _ tion un _ _ r _ o _, in _ ivisi _ l _

with li _ _ rty _ n _ Justi _ _ _ or _ ll.

# My Country 'Tis Of Thee

# The Talking Parakeet

(A **Palindrome** is a song that sounds the same played backwards or forwards)

Here are some familiar words that are palindromes:
MOM, DAD, BOB, LEVEL and RADAR

Gail Smith

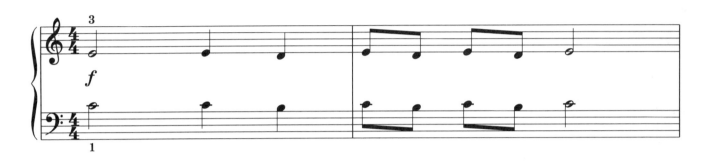

Repeat playing backwards

# Ten Little Indians

This song is a "Semordnilap". It can be played forward and then sounds different when it is played backwards. When you play this song backwards, you will recognize the song as, "Ten Little Indians".

# Little Minuet

Gail Smith

56

# Finding Five Notes

Repeat Five Times

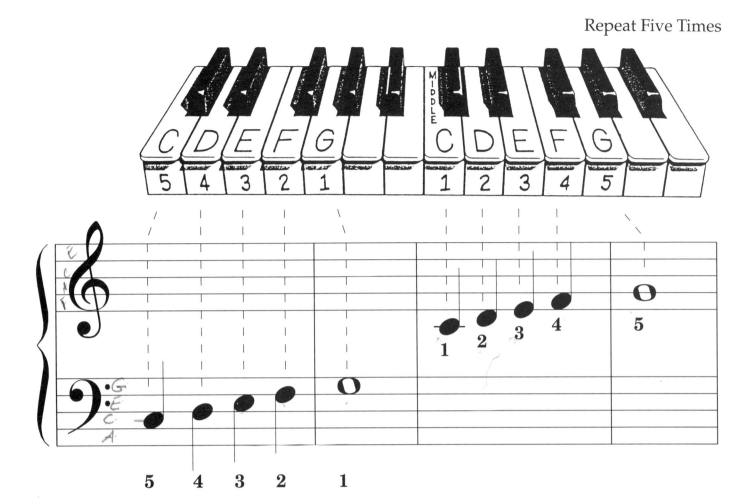

# Look Out For B Flats!

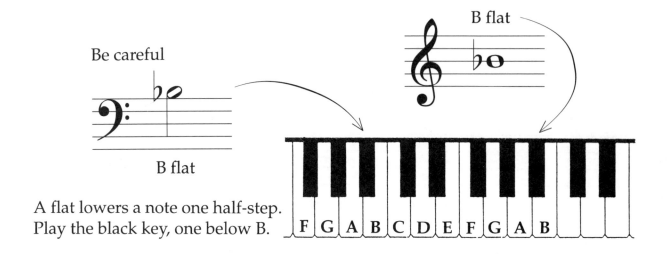

Be careful

B flat

A flat lowers a note one half-step.
Play the black key, one below B.

F G A B C D E F G A B

Find the B flats in the keyboard below and color them blue.

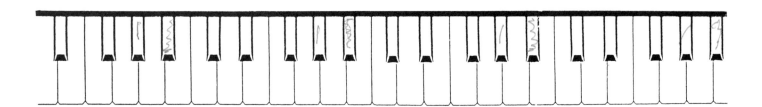

Draw a row of flat signs in both clefs.

58

# The Field Trip

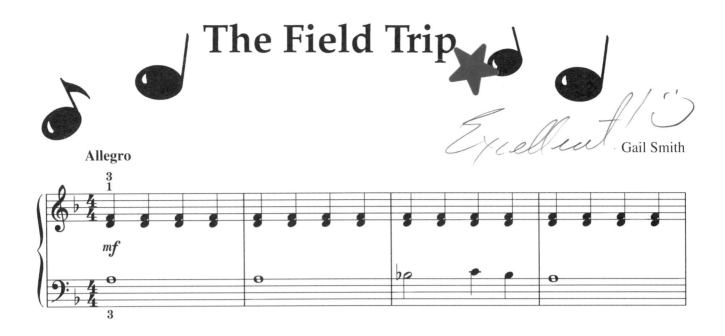

Gail Smith

# ♯ Be Sharp ♯

A sharp raises a note one-half step.

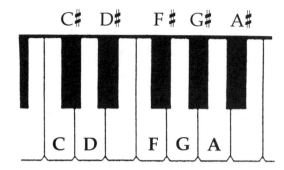

Find every D sharp in the keyboard below and color the note red.

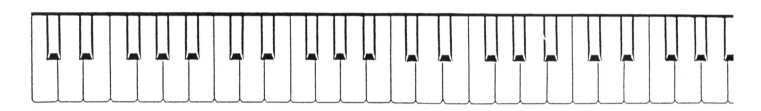

# ♮ Be Natural ♮

A natural sign cancels a sharp or flat and means to play just the white note again.

## Accidentals

In the space below, draw a row of sharps.

Draw a row of the natural signs.

60

# Make Believe It's Beethoven

Arranged by Gail Smith

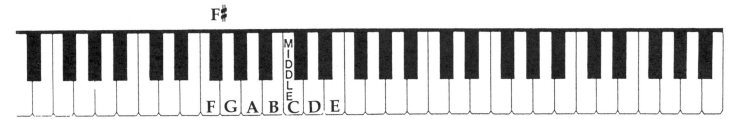

# Jingle Bells

J. Pierpont

F Sharp

62

# Stop, Look And Listen

Gail Smith

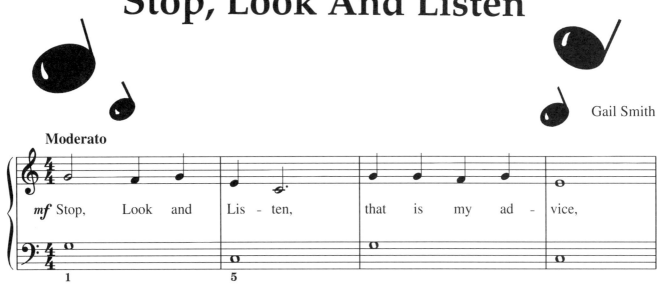

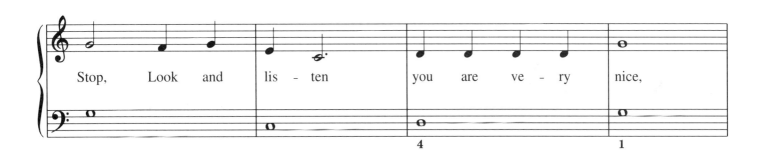

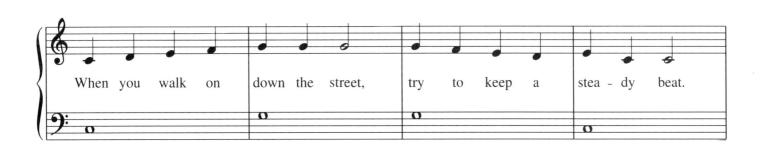

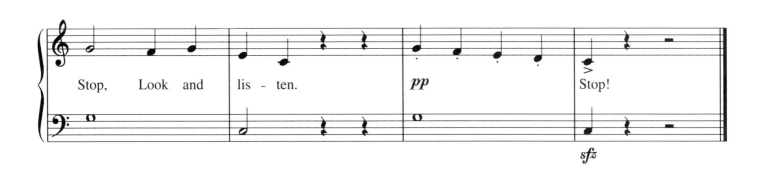

# Finger Exercises

# Three Palindromes

Gail Smith

1.

Ma — dam I'm A - dam

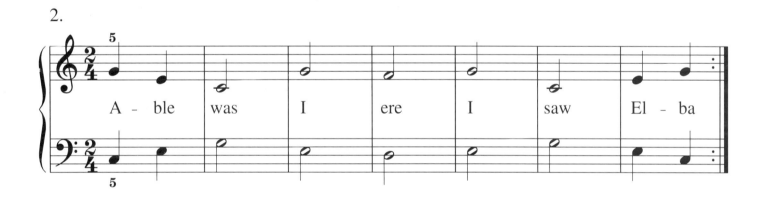

2.

A - ble was I ere I saw El - ba

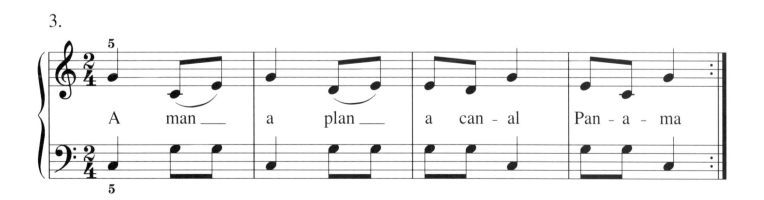

3.

A man ___ a plan ___ a can - al Pan - a - ma

# Canon in F

Op. 14, No. 13

K. M. Kunz

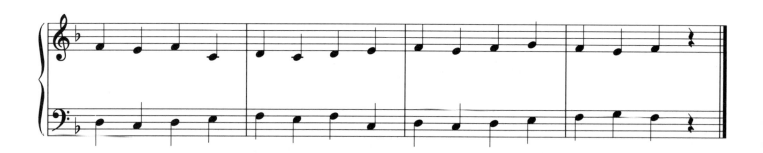

# The Metronome

The metronome helps us keep a steady beat when we play in rhythm to it. It is a device that sounds regular beats at adjustable speeds from slow to fast. The metronome was invented by Johann Nepomuk Maelzel (1772 - 1838). The abbreviation M. M. stands for Maelzel's Metronome. When you see M. M. = 60 for example, it means you will hear 60 clicks per minute. Usually you play one quarter note to a click or two eighth notes to a click. Practice this song with the metronome.

**M.M. = 60**

Gail Smith

This song is a palindrome and can be played backwards and sounds the same as forward. Repeat backwards.

# Do Geese See God?

### A Canon Palindrome

Gail Smith

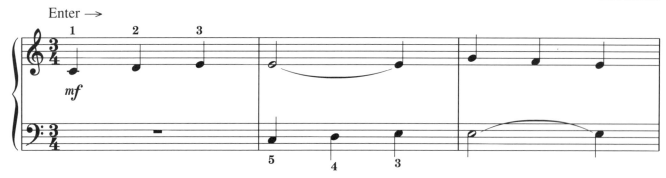

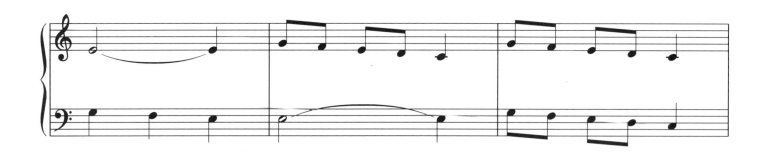

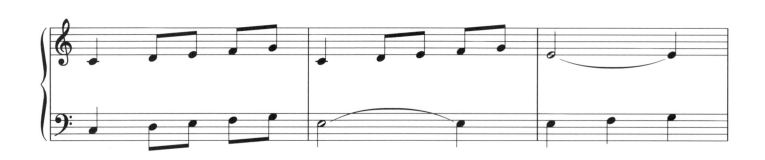

← Exit
*Repeat and play backwards*

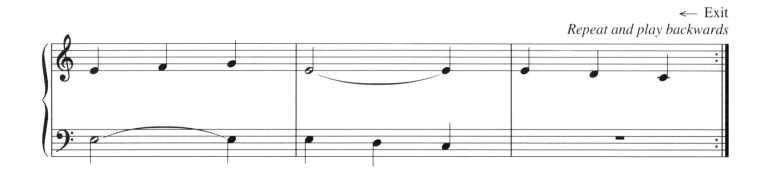

# The Interval Of A Fifth

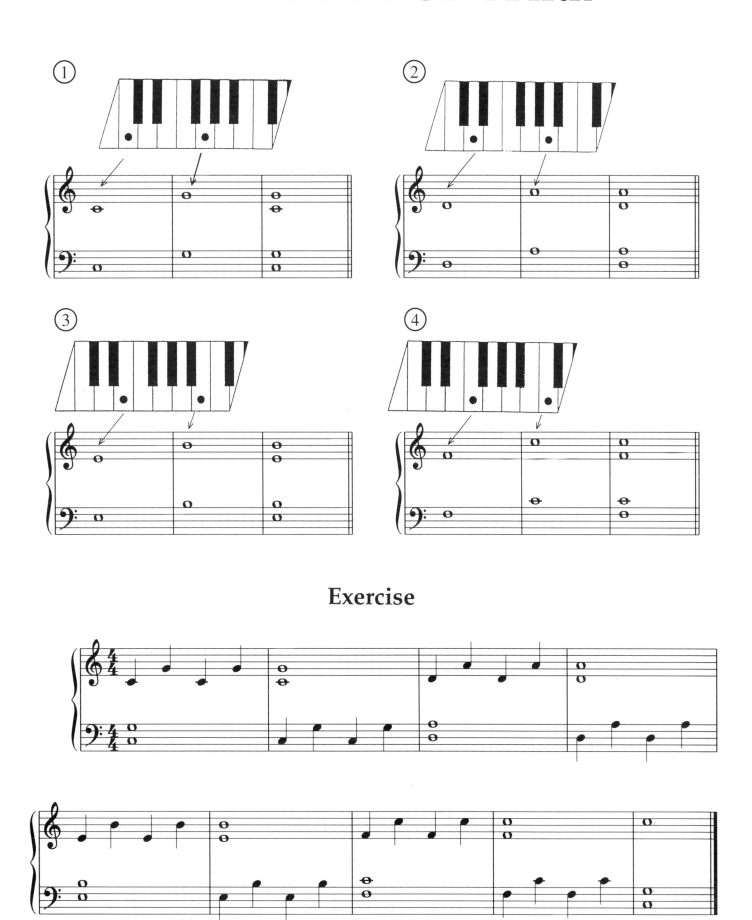

## Exercise

# Footsteps

Gail Smith

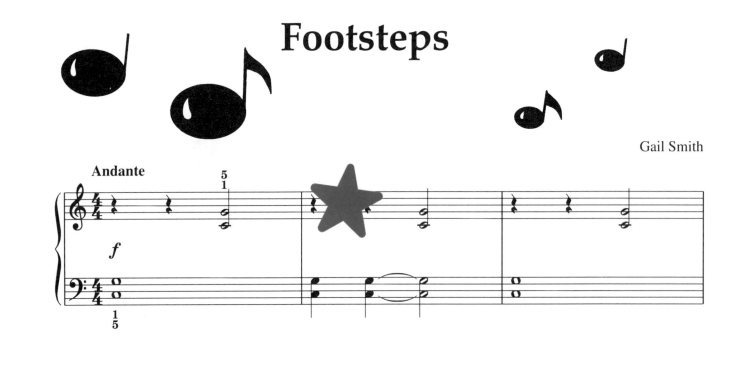

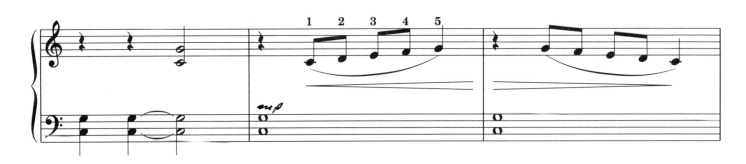

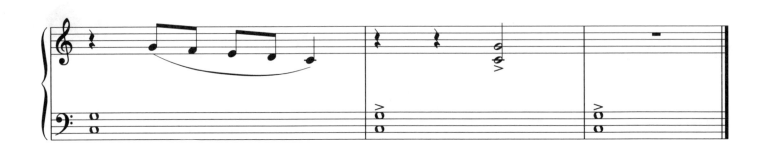

# Happy or Sad Song

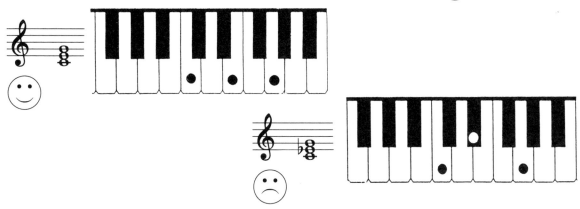

Gail Smith

By the sound of the chord, fill in the face.

Happy for major    Sad for minor

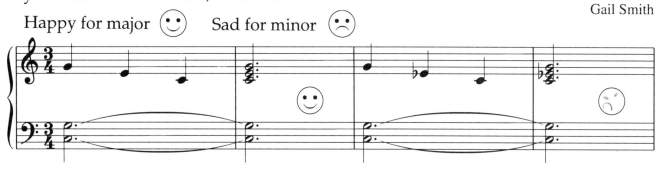

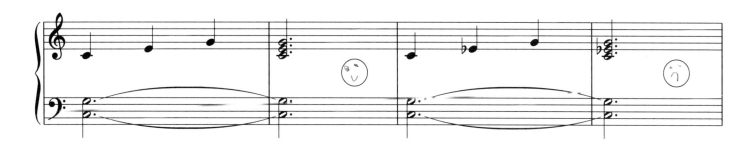

# Nikkanochee Osceola

### Dedicated to Judy Bill Osceola

Gail Smith

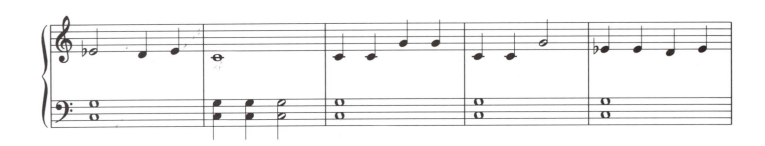

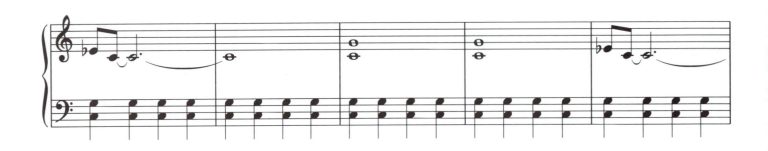

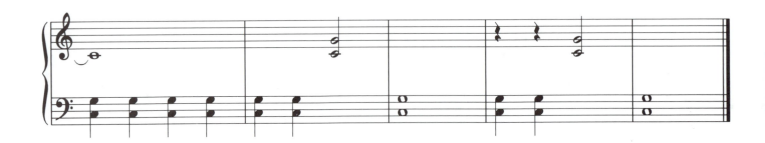

# Handy

Gail Smith

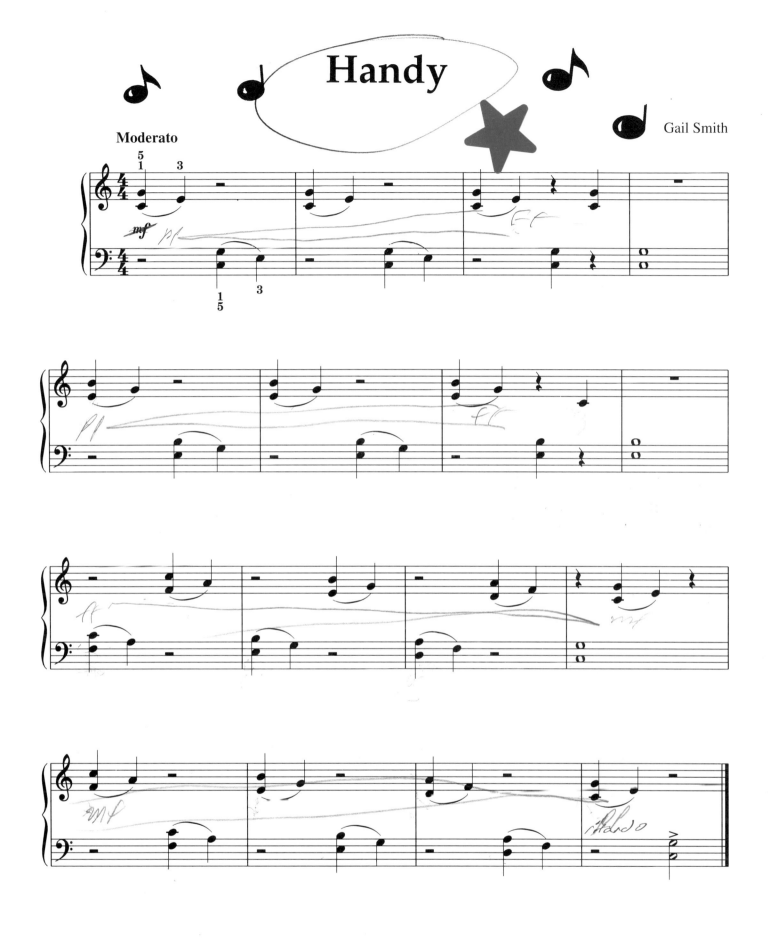

# TRUE OR FALSE QUIZ
Mark T for True or F for False for each of the following questions.

_T_   1. The lines in the Treble Clef are EGBDF.

_F_   2. The spaces in the Treble Clef are ACEG.

_T_   3. The second space in the Bass Clef is C.

_F_   4. The lines in the Bass Clef are FACE.

_T_   5. The second line in the Treble Clef is G.

_T_   6. A whole note gets four beats.

_T_   7. A quarter note gets one beat.

_T_   8. A half note gets a half beat.

_T_   9. This is an eighth note. ♪

_F_   10. *pp* means to play very loud.

_T_   11. *f*  means to play loud.

_T_   12. Allegro means to play fast.

_T_   13. Lento means to play slowly.

_T_   14. These notes step.

_T_   15. These notes skip.

_T_   16. This is a repeat sign. :‖

_T_   17. A dotted half note ( 𝅗𝅥. ) equals three counts.

_F_   18. The Time Signature is at the end of a song.

_F_   19. Staccato means to play very smooth.

_T_   20. Ritard (Rit.) means to play slower.

_T_   21. Haydn composed The Surprise Symphony.

_T_   22. This is a Sharp sign (♯) which raises a note a half step.

_T_   23. This is a Natural sign (♮) which cancels a sharp or flat.

_T_   24. A Palindrome is a song that can be played backwards or forwards and sound the same.

_F_   25. A metronome is a dwarf who lives in the city.